level

3

Robots

Chris Oxlade

KINGFISHER

First published 2017 by Kingfisher
an imprint of Macmillan Children's Books
20 New Wharf Road, London N1 9RR
Associated companies throughout the world
www.panmacmillan.com

Series editor: Hayley Down
Literacy consultant: Hilary Horton
Design: Peter Clayman

ISBN 978-0-7534-4095-7

9 8 7 6 5 4 3 2 1

1TR/0317/WKT/UG/105MA

A CIP catalogue record for this book is available from the British Library.

Printed in China

Picture credits
The Publisher would like to thank the following for permission to reproduce their material.
Top = t; Bottom = b; Centre = c; Left = l; Right = r
Cover NASA; Pages 4 Shutterstock/Photodiem; 5 Getty/Syfy/Contributor; 6l Wikipedia/Creative Commons; 7
Getty/Science & Society Picture Library/Contributor; 8 Getty/ERIC PIERMONT/Staff; 9t iStock/Jaroslav Frank
9b Alamy/Macrocosmos; 10 ABB/new.abb.com; 11 iStock/Alexey Dudoladov; 12 Getty/Junko Kimura/Staff;
13 Getty/Chesnot/Contributor; 14 NASA; 15 Alamy/ MixPix; 16 iStock/RuslanDashinsky; 17t Shutterstock/
avarand, 17b Shutterstock/Thatsaphons; 18 NASA; 19 Getty/Yamaguchi Haruyoshi/Contributor, 20 Getty/Just
Sullivan/Staff; 22–23 Alamy/Xinhua; 24 Shutterstock/Tinxi; 25 iStock; 26 Alamy/age fotostock, 27t Alamy/615
collection, 27b Alamy/WENN Ltd; 28 Getty/Silver Screen Collection, 29 Getty/Kevin Winter.

Contents

What are robots?

What comes into your mind when you hear the word 'robot'? Is it a giant machine from a film? Is it a remote-controlled toy? Or is it a robot working in a car-making factory?

Every robot has a computer that acts like its brain. A **program** in the computer decides how and when the robot moves.

Robot wars!
Some people build
their own robots to
battle for fun.

Robots come in a huge range of shapes and
sizes, and do many different jobs. They work
in factories, in homes, at theme parks, high
in the air and even deep under the sea!

The first robots

Inventors started building simple robots, called **automatons**, 500 years ago. There were automatons that could play musical instruments, write letters and dance. In 1738, a French inventor built a robot duck that flapped its wings, ate food and even quacked!

Robot writer
This automaton, built by inventor Henri Maillardet in 1800, could write and draw pictures!

UN

In 1920, a Czech writer called Karel Capek invented the word 'robot' when he was writing a play. The word comes from the word *robota*, which means 'hard work' in the Czech language.

The first factory robot was called Unimate. It started work in 1961, helping to build cars.

Robots at home

Domestic robots help with jobs in people's homes, while their owners are at work, relaxing or fast asleep! There are robots that can **automatically** clean carpets, sweep floors, wash windows or mow lawns.

Best Buddy!
Helper robots, such as this robot called Buddy, can find information on the Internet and play games with children.

A domestic robot moves across the floor, sucking up dust as it goes. When it reaches

a wall or a piece of furniture, it automatically turns round. It returns to its base station to **recharge** its batteries before they run down.

There is no robot that can do all of the household jobs yet, but there might be one day!

lawn-mowing robot

Factory robots

Most robots are **industrial** ones that work in factories. They lift and move heavy objects; they cut, drill and shape materials using tools; and they tighten screws, nuts and bolts to join things together. Industrial robots work very **accurately**, and never make mistakes.

YuMi robot

Lend a hand!
The incredible YuMi robot works with humans in factories. It moves so accurately that it can fold a paper aeroplane!

An industrial robot has the same parts as a human arm, with a shoulder joint, an elbow joint and a wrist joint. Each joint can bend and twist. Different tools are attached to the end of the arm. For example, a gripper picks up objects, a screwdriver tightens screws and a spray gun sprays paint.

On the move

Your senses, such as touch, sight and hearing, tell you about the world around you. Robots have senses too. A robot might have touch **sensors** that tell it when it has bumped into something, or **proximity** sensors that tell it when another object is nearby. It might also have a video camera to see what's around it, and microphones to **detect** sound.

Moving motors!

Electric motors make a robot's wheels or tracks turn, or its legs lift and bend. The robot's computer switches these motors on and off.

Many robots roll along on wheels or tracks.

Others walk along on legs, sometimes two legs like you do, sometimes four legs, like dogs and cats, and sometimes six or eight legs, like insects and spiders.

Robot explorers

A space **probe** explores other planets and moons in our **solar system**, taking photographs from space. Some probes land on the planet's surface to take a closer look, and some even drive around – to explore! Human controllers back on the Earth operate space probes.

NASA's *Curiosity* **rover** has been on Mars since 2012.

This AUV moves through an obstacle course.

Underwater robots

Remotely operated vehicles, called ROVs, are robots steered by **remote control**. **Autonomous** underwater vehicles, called AUVs, find their own way through the water.

Robots also work deep under the sea! They send back photographs and videos of the seabed, **marine** animals and interesting shipwrecks. They also help to mend oil pipes and underwater cables.

Drones

A **drone** is a flying robot that works as an 'eye in the sky'. It has an on-board video camera to record video pictures, or send them to a screen on a remote-control handset, tablet or computer.

rotor

Lifting up!
Drones have spinning **rotors** that lift them into the air. Smaller, lighter drones have four or more rotors, but larger, heavier drones have six or even eight rotors.

Drones film events, such as football matches, cycle races and music concerts. Other people use them to film themselves and their friends mountain biking, skateboarding or snowboarding.

A drone pilot flies a drone with a remote control. Moving sticks and pressing switches on the controller makes the drone fly up, down, forwards and backwards.

Autonomous drones can fly themselves, using **GPS** to return to their starting point.

Robots that look like us

Scientists and engineers build robots that look like humans, move like humans and even behave like humans!

Humanoid robots are robots that have the same body shape as humans. They have a torso, a head and two arms, but they still look like machines. Some humanoids move on wheels, and some walk on legs.

Androids look exactly like humans!
An android has lifelike skin, and a face
that smiles and frowns. Androids can
also talk, and some can answer simple
questions. One day in the future,
it may be hard to tell humans and
androids apart!

Otonaroid, a
Japanese android

To the rescue

Some robots do jobs that would be too dangerous for humans. We send robots to examine bags, cars or trucks that might contain hidden bombs. An expert operates the robot with a remote control. The robot carries tools to destroy bombs.

bomb-disposal robot

Fire-fighting robots help firefighters to put out flames. The robots go into places where it would be too hot or smoky for humans to go. Firefighters also fly drones above burning buildings, using their **infrared cameras** to show where the hottest parts of a fire are.

Robot sports and games

Some people build robots as a hobby. They build robots to play football, chess, snooker and other games. Scientists and engineers also build sports robots to test how clever they can make robots at moving, playing games and working in teams.

The RoboCup is an annual football tournament for robots. The robots play in teams, passing the ball to each other and trying to score goals. They couldn't beat human football players, but they are getting better each year!

Robot toys

Toyshops often have robots on display! Toy-makers started making toy robots nearly 100 years ago. There are toy humanoid robots, robot vehicles, robot pets and monsters, walking robots, talking robots and robots from sci-fi films.

Learning is fun!
Robot toys are great for learning about science, technology, engineering and maths.

Some robot toys have
sensors such as cameras and
microphones, and can react
to movements and sounds.
These robots are controlled
by **apps** on tablets
or smartphones.

⭐ **Cool kits**
A robotics kit
contains all the
parts needed to
build an interesting
robot, including
sensors, controllers
and motors.

Robots in battle

Military robots help armies and air forces on the battlefield and in the air. They spy on enemy forces, which would be a dangerous job for soldiers and pilots.

a military drone filming   camera

Military drones are also called unmanned aerial vehicles, or UAVs. They take photos and film as they fly — some even carry **missiles** to fire.

Small spy robots travel across rough ground on tracks, operated by a soldier with a remote control. The robot sends pictures of enemy positions back to the soldier.

Big Dog!
This robot can carry heavy loads across a bumpy battlefield.

Robots on screen

Film-makers design fantastic robots
for their films. These robots can be
frightening or friendly, miniature or
giant, and can have incredible powers!
Film-makers make detailed models
of the robots or create robots with
computer-generated imagery
(called **CGI** for short).

Robots started
appearing in films
in the 1920s. A giant
alien robot called Gort
stepped out of a flying
saucer in a 1951 film
called *The Day the
Earth Stood Still*.

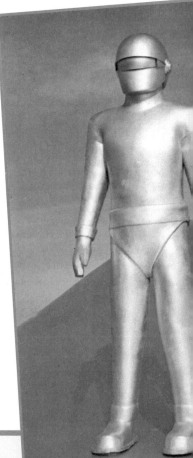

The two most famous film robots are R2-D2 and C-3PO from the *Star Wars* series. C-3PO is a gold-coloured humanoid robot that is programmed to always be polite to humans.

Giant Gort
Gort was played by an actor who was 2.3 metres tall and wore a foam suit!

Glossary

accurately without any mistakes.

android a robot that looks exactly like a human.

app a program found on smartphones or laptops.

automatically working on its own.

automaton a mechanical human or animal, such as a robot, with parts that move.

autonomous something that works on its own.

CGI short for computer-generated imagery, images that are drawn by computer.

detect to notice something using the senses.

drone a flying robot.

GPS short for Global Positioning System, a system that uses satellites to find places on the Earth.

humanoid a robot that is shaped like a human.

industrial works in a factory.

infrared camera a camera that can see heat and helps to find very hot parts of a burning building.

marine from the sea.

missile a weapon that is fired at faraway places.

probe a robot sent to space for research.

program instructions that a computer carries out.

proximity how close an object is to something.

recharge to put electric charge into a battery.

remote-control a way of controlling a robot by moving sticks and pressing buttons on a handset.

rotor part of a machine that turns around, such as a helicopter's blades.

rover a type of robot that works on the surface of a planet, moon or comet.

sensor a device that finds out about the world around it, such as a video camera.

solar system a star and all of the objects that orbit (or circle) it.

Index